D0167379

The Story of

BANKER OF THE PEOPLE

MUHAMMAD YUNUS

To Professor Muhammad Yunus and his commitment to eradicating poverty from our world so no child will go to sleep hungry —P.Y.

For Mich, P., and Bean —J.A.

The author would like to thank the following people for their help and support: Jason Low; Emily Hazel; my wonderful editor, Jessica Echeverria; Steven Malk; Mark Mancall, Professor of History, Emeritus, Stanford University; Simi Singh Juneja; and Ajmal Sobhan. Special thanks to Professor Muhammad Yunus; Hans Reitz, founder and managing director of Grameen Creative Lab; and everyone at the Yunus Centre, including Executive Director Lamiya Morshed, program officers Sharmen Shahria Ferdush and Shiban Mahbub, and program associate Md. Robayt Khondoker.

The Story of
BANKER OF THE PEOPLE
MUHAMMAD YUNUS

by **Paula Yoo**

illustrated by **Jamel Akib**

with additional material by **A. M. Dassu**

Lee & Low Books Inc.
New York

Text copyright © 2014 by Paula Yoo
Illustrations copyright © 2014 by Jamel Akib
Sidebar material by A. M. Dassu © 2019 by Lee & Low Books Inc.
Photo credits: p. 15: Classic Image / Alamy Stock Photo • p. 19: © World Scout Bureau
Inc. • p. 24: Pictorial Press Ltd. / Alamy Stock Photo • p. 26: Map by NeuStudio ©
2019 by Lee & Low Books Inc. • p. 27 World History Archive / Ann Ronan Collection /
Agefotostock • p. 38 public domain • p. 46 Insight-Photography / Shutterstock.com •
p. 48 Hadrian / Shutterstock.com. • p. 49 ID 72137488 © Samrat35 | Dreamstime.com
• p. 61 public domain • p. 63 catwalker / Shutterstock.com • p. 68: Nasir Ali Mamun /
Yunus Centre

LEE & LOW BOOKS Inc., 95 Madison Avenue, New York, NY 10016
leeandlow.com
Edited by Jessica Echeverria and Cheryl Klein
Book design by Charice Silverman and NeuStudio
Book production by The Kids at Our House
The text is set in Vollkorn and Avenir
The illustrations are rendered in chalk pastel
Cataloging-in-Publication data is on file with the Library of Congress.
ISBN 978-1-64379-006-0

10 9 8 7 6 5 4 3 2 1
First Edition

TABLE OF CONTENTS

CHAPTER ONE
A HAPPY CHILDHOOD

Muhammad's stomach growled as he and his brothers and sisters watched their mother mix rice flour, sugar, and coconut to create the dough for sweet *pithas*. She molded the dough into oval cakes and dropped them into hot oil. Each pitha floated to the top of the pan, frying to a crispy golden brown. Then she placed the pithas on a plate to cool.

Eight-year-old Muhammad eagerly reached for a pitha. But before he could take his first bite, someone knocked on the door. Outside stood a **weary** woman and a little girl. The woman said they hadn't eaten in days.

Poor people often stopped by the house because Muhammad's mother was known for giving away food, money, and even clothes her children had outgrown. Muhammad knew the hungry people at the door needed the food more than he did. He placed the pitha back on the plate. His mother smiled at him as the grateful woman and child ate every crumb.

Muhammad Yunus was born on June 28, 1940, the third oldest of nine children. His **Bengali** family lived in a two-story house in the port city of Chittagong, then part of India. Chittagong was a bustling city. Delivery trucks rumbled past passengers riding in colorful **rickshaws.** Beggars wandered side by side with businessmen along the densely crowded streets. People sipped tea or ate *chanachur*, a snack made of fried lentils and chickpeas, at one of the tea stalls along the roads.

Muhammad and his siblings found many ways to have fun together. They pretended to be soldiers, chasing one another across the flat rooftop of their house. They flew kites made of bamboo and paper. And sometimes after school they were allowed to go to the movies.

Education was very important to Muhammad's parents, and they made sure their children studied very hard. Although Muhammad's father, Dula Mia, was a successful jewelry maker, he had just an eighth-grade education. Muhammad's mother, Sofia Khatun, went to school only up to the fourth grade, but she was passionate about

CHAPTER TWO

LEARNING FROM THE WORLD

Dula Mia also encouraged his sons to explore the world by joining organizations such as the Boy Scouts. "Learning from the world is the greatest learning," he told them.

> "Learning from the world is the greatest learning."

Muhammad liked being a Boy Scout. The boys played games, hiked in the countryside, mastered outdoor scouting skills, and worked to help the less fortunate in their community. During some scout outings, Muhammad saw the terrible conditions in the **slums** where poor people lived. Families were crammed into tiny **shanties** built of bamboo, cardboard, and rusted tin. Homeless mothers huddled with their children in alleyways overflowing with **sewage**. It was almost impossible for the families to find enough fresh water and clean food.

Muhammad became very active in his troop's charity activities. The Scouts hosted Earnings Weeks during which they polished boots and sold books and tea to raise money for the poor. Muhammad noticed how just a few coins could buy enough rice to feed a family for an entire week.

As he grew older, Muhammad wanted to continue helping those who were living in **poverty.** In 1957, at the age of seventeen, he enrolled in the Department of Economics at Dhaka University. Economics is the study of how people make and use money, goods, and services. Muhammad thought studying economics would teach him how to help the poor manage and save their money better.

After graduating from Dhaka University, Muhammad became a research assistant and lecturer. Then in 1965 he won a **prestigious** Fulbright scholarship to study economics in the United States. While in America, he witnessed college students holding peace rallies to show their opposition to the **Vietnam War**. They went

The Boy Scouts

Robert S.S. Baden-Powell in the late 1890s.

The Scouts Movement was founded in 1908 in Great Britain by Robert S.S. Baden-Powell. He was a **cavalry** officer who served in the British colony in South Africa. During a seven-month **siege** in the **Second Boer War**, between October 1899 and May 1900, Baden-Powell gave boys jobs to do, such as delivering messages, assisting soldiers, helping in hospitals, and acting as lookouts. Baden-Powell realized that young people, when challenged, worked well under pressure.

After he returned to Britain, Baden-Powell wanted to tap into the potential of young people in the country. In 1907, he invited twenty boys—some wealthy and some from working-class homes—to a camp on Brownsea Island, off the coast of southern England, to test his ideas for a new training program. Baden-Powell organized the boys into small troops. The oldest boy in each patrol was given the role of Patrol Leader, and he was responsible for his patrol's behavior in camp and in the field.

Scouts were rewarded with badges for mastering skills such as lighting a fire, cooking supper, and making shelters. The training got more challenging as boys learned new skills. Boys had to carry out at least one good deed every day, and medals were awarded for heroic acts, such as saving someone from drowning. The activities and challenges the Scouts experienced developed their physical, emotional, spiritual, social, and thinking skills.

Around the same time, Baden-Powell rewrote *Aids to Scouting*, a popular book he'd written for soldiers, so it would be appropriate for children. *Scouting for Boys* was published in 1908. It included tips on health and **hygiene,** lessons in **woodcraft,** adventure tales, natural history, a first-aid guide, games, and much more. It also contained the first version of the "Scout Law," which is a code of courageous and polite conduct. The most recent edition of the Scout Law reads:

A Scout is trustworthy, loyal, helpful, friendly, courteous, kind, obedient, cheerful, thrifty, brave, clean, and reverent.

Scouts were encouraged to do their duty to God, to themselves, and in particular, to other people, and to always be prepared to do the right thing at the right time.

Scouting for Boys had such a powerful effect that boys started forming Scout troops unexpectedly all over Britain. So many inquiries came in about Scouting that Baden-Powell had to set up an office to deal with them! The "Boy Scouts Movement" spread fast: by 1910, there were Scout troops in Sweden, Mexico, Argentina, Canada, Australia, South Africa, and the United States.

The Boy Scouts Movement was originally planned for boys aged eleven and over, but the demand was so great for similar programs for younger boys that Baden-Powell founded the Wolf Cubs (known as Cub Scouts in some countries) in 1916. In 1910, Baden-Powell's sister, Agnes Baden-Powell, founded the Girl Guides, which became known as the Girl Scouts in the United States. Ten years later, the first Scout World **Jamboree**, or international Scout meeting, was held in London. Since then, a Jamboree has been held every four years, bringing together thousands of Scouts to represent their countries and camp together.

The Scouts now have more than fifty million members and are established in almost every country around the world. In 2018, the Boy Scouts of America (BSA)

A Muslim Scout learns a traditional Japanese dance at the 2015 World Scout Jamboree in western Japan.

announced that the Boy Scouting program would be renamed "Scouts BSA" and would admit girls as well as boys at all levels.

In his final message to the Scouts, Baden-Powell said: "The real way to get happiness is by giving out happiness to other people. Try and leave this world a little better than you found it."

CHAPTER THREE

UPHEAVAL

In 1970 Muhammad accepted a teaching job at Middle Tennessee State University. Although he was happy in the United States, Muhammad worried about the **turmoil** in his home country.

When British rule of India ended in 1947, Chittagong became part of what was known as East Bengal and later East Pakistan. The region was home to a large Bengali population. Due to economic, political, and cultural differences, the people of East Pakistan wanted their independence from the West Pakistani government. In March 1971 East Pakistan **seceded** and declared itself the independent nation of Bangladesh. Tensions continued to mount, soon leading to a war between Pakistan and the new nation of Bangladesh.

Inspired to support his people, Muhammad organized rallies on the university campus. He also went to Washington, DC, where he and other Bengalis demonstrated on the steps of Capitol Hill. They chanted for peace between Bangladesh and Pakistan. They answered questions for television and newspaper reporters to raise awareness about the situation in their homeland.

Bangladesh eventually defeated Pakistan, and the brutal war was declared over on December 16, 1971. An estimated three hundred thousand people had been killed. The war, along with drought and **famine**, devastated the newly formed country.

Muhammad realized it was time to return to Bangladesh. In 1972 he set out for home and accepted a job as head of the Economics Department at Chittagong University.

The Partition of India and the Creation of Bangladesh

In the fifteenth century, traders from England, France, the Netherlands, Portugal, and Spain began exploring the world, looking for valuable goods. The first of these explorers arrived in India in the late 1400s. They bought black pepper, cinnamon, and cloves, and then sold these spices in Europe. Back then, spices were as valuable as gold, so the explorers made a great deal of money, and decided to stay in India and **colonize** it.

The British successfully fought the other countries doing business in India and won control of India's international trade. Indians enlisted as soldiers in the British Army, and in 1858 India became part of the British Empire. However, Indians were unhappy with the amount of control the British had over their country and its resources, and in the early 1900s many began campaigning for independence from the British.

Tensions grew after World War I. More than a million Indian soldiers fought in the British Army during the war, and they expected more power in India in return for their service. When that didn't happen, and the British killed protesters during a peaceful meeting in the city of Amritsar in 1919, **Mohandas Gandhi** began a nonviolent campaign against the British colonizers. He asked Indians to **boycott** British goods and challenge any laws that **discriminated** against them. The movement to gain independence continued until 1947, when the British announced they would withdraw from India.

From left to right: Muhammad Ali Jinnah, leader of the Muslim League and first Governor-General of Pakistan, and Mohandas Gandhi in 1944.

The struggle for independence had made existing religious tensions between **Hindus** and **Muslims** worse. The majority of people in India were Hindus, and the country's Muslims were afraid of a Hindu government ruling over them. During the independence **negotiations**, they asked for a separate country of their own. After extreme violence increased between Hindus and Muslims, British and Indian leaders agreed to divide the **subcontinent** into separate nations.

On August 15, 1947, India finally gained its independence from the British, and a process called Partition began. India was split into two separate nations: India, which was intended to be primarily Hindu, and Pakistan, a Muslim country divided into two states that were nearly a thousand miles apart. The name "Pakistan" came from the initials of several provinces that made up the state of West Pakistan, including **P**unjab, **A**fghan Province, **K**ashmir, **S**ind, and Baluch**istan**. East Pakistan had been formerly known as the Indian province of Eastern Bengal.

To stay with the people who shared their religion,

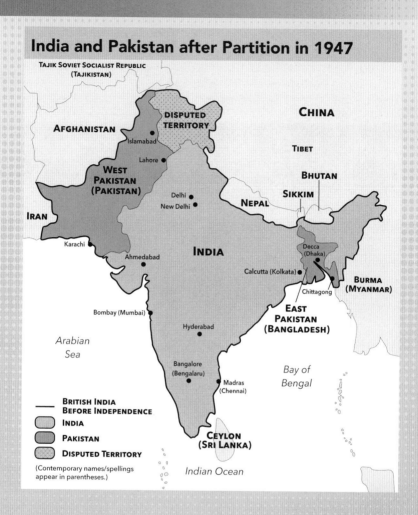

India and Pakistan after Partition in 1947

TAJIK SOVIET SOCIALIST REPUBLIC
(TAJIKISTAN)

AFGHANISTAN

DISPUTED TERRITORY

CHINA

Islamabad

Lahore

TIBET

WEST PAKISTAN
(PAKISTAN)

Delhi
New Delhi

BHUTAN

SIKKIM

NEPAL

IRAN

Karachi

INDIA

Decca
(Dhaka)

Ahmedabad

Calcutta (Kolkata)

BURMA
(MYANMAR)

Chittagong

Bombay (Mumbai)

Hyderabad

EAST PAKISTAN
(BANGLADESH)

Arabian
Sea

Bangalore
(Bengalaru)

Bay of
Bengal

Madras
(Chennai)

BRITISH INDIA
BEFORE INDEPENDENCE

INDIA

PAKISTAN

DISPUTED TERRITORY

CEYLON
(SRI LANKA)

(Contemporary names/spellings
appear in parentheses.)

Indian Ocean

many Muslims in India had to settle into the new Pakistan, and Hindus and **Sikhs** in Pakistan were expected to travel into India. But Partition was not organized well. The border lines that would divide the two countries were rushed through by the British

26

Two young men sit on a hill above a refugee camp near Delhi, India, during Partition in 1947.

and finalized less than a week before Partition officially began. Fifteen million people left their homes overnight—the largest mass migration in human history—and between one and two million people were killed in the resulting violence.

The troubles continued as **refugees** settled into their new lands and the countries became more established. East Pakistan disliked being controlled by West Pakistan, which was richer and more powerful, even though it had a smaller population. In 1952, the government based in West Pakistan declared Urdu the official language of the entire state. The people in East Pakistan spoke Bengali rather than Urdu, and violent **demonstrations** erupted around the country.

Throughout the 1960s, East Pakistanis remained frustrated with their lack of representation in the Pakistani government and the amount of money spent on their part of the country. In 1971, civil war broke out after Sheikh Mujibur Rahman from East Pakistan won Pakistan's general election but was prevented from becoming **prime minister** of both states. After almost 9.5 million refugees fled across its border because of the violence, India finally stepped in to help East Pakistan militarily. Within two weeks, West Pakistan surrendered, and the new country of Bangladesh was created on December 16, 1971.

CHAPTER FOUR

TWENTY-TWO CENTS

Now Muhammad saw firsthand how the war had affected his country. Every morning on his way to the university, he drove by the village of Jobra. The drought had destroyed the crops and left the villagers without food and fresh water. Barefoot children and their parents **trudged** along the dirt road toward the nearby **fertile** hills in desperate attempts to find food. Some returned clutching a few precious handfuls of rice and twigs to eat.

Muhammad was **frustrated** by all this poverty. Why was he teaching economics in a classroom when so many people in the village were suffering? Jobra became his new classroom. Over the next few years he interviewed many families so he could understand how they were surviving on very little.

In 1976 Muhammad met a young woman named Sufiya Begum. Her children slept in a mud hut while she wove bamboo into beautiful stools. She was weak and thin from lack of food, but the artistry of her work greatly impressed Muhammad.

Muhammad learned that Sufiya was one of many women who sold their crafts at the market to support their families. The bamboo used to make stools cost five **taka**, about twenty-two cents. Sufiya did not have twenty-two cents, so she had to borrow the money.

The banks in Jobra were not interested in loaning small amounts of money, and they did not want to risk making loans to poor people. So Sufiya had to go to a *mahajon*, a moneylender. The mahajon loaned her the twenty-two cents she needed, which she had to pay back with interest, a percentage of the amount she borrowed. But the

mahajon took advantage of Sufiya and charged an unfairly high interest rate on her loan.

interest (IN-tur-est) *noun* (1) the amount a bank pays to a customer in order to hold the customer's money; (2) the amount a bank charges a customer for a loan

interest rate (IN-tur-est rait) *noun* the number that determines how much interest the bank will pay or charge, usually a percentage of the total sum held by the bank or borrowed by the customer.

After Sufiya sold her stools and paid off her loan plus the interest, she was usually left with only two cents for herself. Two cents was not enough money to buy more bamboo. Two cents was not enough money to buy food for her family. As a result, Sufiya was forced to borrow more money from the mahajon.

Muhammad realized that Sufiya's life depended on just a few cents a day. He reached into his pocket. It jingled with many coins. He could easily give Sufiya the twenty-two cents she needed to buy more bamboo. Then she wouldn't owe the mahajon anything and could keep all the **profits** for herself.

But Muhammad hesitated. If he gave Sufiya the money, she would always be dependent on strangers for charity. Giving her the twenty-two cents would not solve her problems in the long run. He needed to figure out a way to help Sufiya and others in her situation break out of the cycle of poverty.

The next day Muhammad took a group of his students to Jobra. There they found forty-two

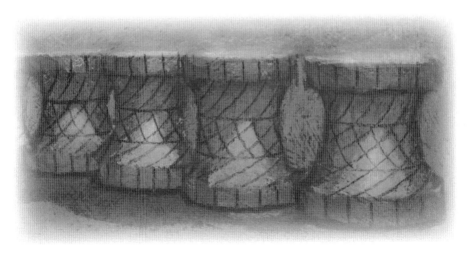

women who needed a total of 856 taka—the **equivalent** of about twenty-seven dollars—to pay off their debts.

Muhammad then visited one of the largest banks in Bangladesh to ask for a loan with a fair interest rate for the women. The bank manager laughed at his request. Twenty-seven dollars was too small an amount for the bank to lend. And because the women were poor and did not know how to read and write, the bank did not trust them to pay back the loan.

The women had the same rights as everyone else, Muhammad believed. If the bank refused to help them, how could the women ever find a way to better their lives?

How Banks Make Money

Banks have two main purposes. They hold money for customers, keeping it safer than, for example, hiding it under a mattress at home. Banks also lend money to customers, allowing them to make large purchases and **investments** for a better quality of life or more income. In both of these situations, banks use interest to calculate how much to pay or charge their customers.

People put their money in banks because it provides a good investment as well as security. Money in a bank account earns interest each month. The longer customers leave their money in an account, and the more money they put in, the more it earns.

Jamie puts $100 into his bank account. The bank sets a 2% annual interest rate. If Jamie leaves $100 in his account for a year, by the end of the year, Jamie will have earned:

$100 x 2% (.02) = $2

That will be added on to the original $100, so Jamie will now have $102 in his account.

To balance their costs and remain successful, banks then loan out the money people have saved with them to other customers, such as homebuyers, businesses, or **entrepreneurs**. Banks charge these customers interest for lending them money.

Jo needs to borrow $1,000. The bank agrees and sets a 10% annual interest rate. The total interest on the loan will be:

$$\$1,000 \times 10\% \; (.10) = \$100$$

That $100 in interest will be added on to the $1,000 **principal** of her loan. So Jo will get $1,000 now, but she will have to pay back $1,100 at the end of the year.

To make a profit, banks charge a higher interest rate on the money they loan than the interest rate they pay the customers saving with them. In the above examples, the bank charged Jo 10 percent interest on her loan and paid out 2 percent interest to Jamie for saving with them, so the difference of 8 percent went towards the bank's overall profit. Banks also charge customers fees for late payments, for using their bank cards abroad, or for overdrafts, when customers take out more money than they have in their accounts. Fees can make banks a lot of money.

Since the **Great Depression** in the 1930s, banks have been required to keep a *capital reserve*, which is a large sum of money that they are not allowed to loan out or invest elsewhere. A capital reserve is necessary in case a lot of customers withdraw money at the same time, or borrowers do not pay their loans back. If a bank lends out too much money and doesn't have enough in reserve, they can borrow more from the *central bank*, which is a national bank that serves a country's government. The central bank in the United States is called the Federal Reserve Bank.

Because the Federal Reserve prints all the cash in the United States, its seal appears on all bills.

CHAPTER FIVE

THE VILLAGE BANK

After being turned down by several banks, Muhammad decided to start a new bank that would lend money to the poor. In 1977 he launched Grameen Bank, which means "village bank" in the Bangla language of Bangladesh.

At Grameen Bank, borrowers could take out loans of very small amounts of money with low interest rates. These small loans became known as *microcredit*. Borrowers would be divided into groups of five, and each group would borrow an agreed-upon amount. Then the group members would work together to pay back their loan on time. Muhammad believed that placing borrowers in groups would create a support system by which an entire group would be responsible

for the success of each member.

At first it was difficult for Muhammad and his students to get women to sign up for his bank's loan program. The women did not understand how Muhammad's way of loaning money would be different from dealing with the mahajons.

Sometimes Muhammad and his students were also **hindered** by the rules of **purdah**, a practice that does not allow women to be seen

interacting with men who are not their husbands. Often Muhammad could not approach a woman in public or in her home because it would be disrespectful. So he waited in the distance or outside a house while one of his female students talked to the women. On some days Muhammad waited patiently for hours in the pouring rain.

The patience and persistence of Muhammad and his students eventually paid off. They won the trust of the women, and many of them signed up for Grameen Bank's loan program.

At the bank the women learned to manage their finances. Each group took a seven-day training course to learn how banking worked. Over time, the women in the course developed a set of important lessons, the Sixteen Decisions, that all participants had to memorize and follow. The lessons taught the women how to change

their lives for the better by providing practical advice about positive habits such as drinking safely boiled water and making sure their children went to school.

To be approved for a loan, each group had to pass a test showing that the women understood

the loan program. The women studied very hard and eventually everyone passed the test. Muhammad smiled as Sufiya clutched her group's loan of twenty-seven dollars as if it were a precious jewel.

Sufiya used her share of the loan to buy ingredients to cook sweets and materials to decorate **bangles** that she could sell alongside her bamboo stools at the market. She earned even more money than before, which was enough to pay back her portion of the loan and still provide for her family. She beamed with pride when she bought rice for her children with her hard-earned money.

The Sixteen Decisions

The Sixteen Decisions are a set of rules that all borrowers at Muhammad Yunus's Grameen Bank must follow. Borrowers are organized into small groups of five members, who work together as a unit called a *centre*.

Women borrowers created and introduced the rules at a workshop in 1984, with the goal of improving the world in which borrowers and their families live, and creating a community in which people work together and help one another. The rules have since become an important part of Grameen Bank's mission.

1.0 We shall follow and advance the four principles of Grameen Bank — <u>Discipline,</u> Unity, Courage, and Hard Work — in all walks of our lives.

2.0 <u>Prosperity</u> we shall bring to our families.

3.0 We shall not live in <u>dilapidated</u> houses. We shall repair our houses and work towards constructing new houses at the earliest.

Most villagers live in small homes made of bamboo or mud, which can be severely affected in times of flooding. Borrowers must aim to have better housing with tin roofs, where each family member sleeps on a bed and not the floor. Better shelters mean better health for borrowers, which gives them the ability to work harder and eventually escape poverty.

Bangladeshi women hold organic potatoes just after a harvest.

4.0   We shall grow vegetables all the year round. We shall eat plenty of them and sell the <u>surplus.</u>

5.0 During the plantation seasons, we shall plant as many seedlings as possible.

Borrowers are reminded to make the most of the seasons and the fertile farmland they live on, instead of just focusing on income from elsewhere. If they plant as much as possible, they can have plenty of good food for themselves and make extra money from selling the food they do not need.

6.0 We shall plan to keep our families small. We shall minimize our expenditures. We shall look after our health.

Many homes in Bangladesh only have one or two rooms, and they are usually crowded with large families living together. Borrowers are encouraged to have fewer children because it is easier to provide food, health care, and comfort for a small family. Grameen Bank expects that no family member should go hungry and everyone should be able to see a doctor if they need to. Borrowers must also use mosquito nets and wear warm clothing during the winter to stay healthy.

7.0 We shall educate our children and ensure that they can earn to pay for their education.

In Bangladesh, primary education is only free for children up to age eleven. Anything beyond that has to be paid for. Borrowers are encouraged to send all children over six years old to school. If children are allowed to go to school, they are more likely to want to study further, which will help them get better jobs and ease their families' financial burdens.

8.0 We shall always keep our children and the environment clean.

9.0 We shall build and use <u>pit latrines</u>.

An ancient Roman pit latrine in Ephesus, Turkey.

In rural areas, people often don't have access to toilets or sewage systems. When it rains, human waste that is left out in the open can wash into the water and cause illness and disease. A pit latrine lets people deposit their waste in a pit deep underground and then keeps this waste contained.

Two children in a village in India drink water from a tubewell.

10.0 We shall drink water from tubewells. If it is not available, we shall boil water or use alum.

A poisonous **element** called arsenic infects much of the water in Bangladesh. Borrowers and their families are asked to drink pure water from deep wells, boil it, or **purify** it with alum or through a pitcher with filters. *Alum* is a chemical mixture that contains aluminum and comes in the form of crystals or powder.

11.0 We shall not take any dowry at our sons' weddings, neither shall we give any dowry at our daughters' weddings. We shall keep our centre free from the curse of dowry. We shall not practice child marriage.

It is still common in some cultures and in rural societies for a boy's family to ask for money from a girl's family before they agree to their marriage—a payment known as a *dowry*. Poorer women are seen as undesirable, so girls' families are under a huge amount of pressure to provide a large dowry. Because this money could be spent on food, housing, and health care, borrowers at Grameen Bank are asked to stop giving away their income or taking others' wealth through the dowry system. This will reduce the burden on families so they can improve their lifestyles.

Similarly, in some cultures, children are married off young in order to pass the cost involved in feeding a child (usually a girl) to another family. Married children are often left uneducated and unable to get good jobs and escape the cycle of poverty. These cultural practices are unfair and increase **inequality**.

12.0 We shall not <u>inflict</u> any injustice on anyone, neither shall we allow anyone to do so.

13.0 We shall <u>collectively</u> undertake bigger investments for higher incomes.

If borrowers work together and invest in more goods, they have more bargaining power and in return more income. For example, if a woman only has twenty taka, and she uses it to buy a spool of thread and some fabric from a shop owner, she will be able to sew only one cloth bag with it—not making her much money. However, ten people can collectively buy ten spools of thread and more fabric, and because they are buying a lot more from the shop owner at one time, he will give them a discount. The women can now sew twenty cloth bags at a cheaper cost, and sell them at different village markets to earn more income.

14.0 We shall always be ready to help each other. If anyone is in difficulty, we shall all help him or her.

Borrowers must work together to make sure that the money lent to them by Grameen Bank is repaid. If one of them is struggling and the others help, they will all be able to repay their loans more quickly, and trustworthy business relationships will be formed. This rule again focuses on improving whole communities and societies, not just one household at a time.

15.0 If we come to know of any <u>breach</u> of discipline in any centre, we shall all go there and help restore discipline.

This rule encourages borrowers to take pride in their work and make sure that no one's behavior will affect all the borrowers' reputations. If borrowers take responsibility for one another, they will be able to continue to build their businesses and achieve more.

16.0 We shall take part in all social activities collectively.

If borrowers all work together, help one another, and then spend their free time together as well, their families form close friendships, and their communities are strengthened.

These rules have proven to be a huge success. Studies have shown that families of Grameen Bank customers are more likely to be healthier; their children are more likely to go to school and on to college; and their household members are more likely to eat three meals a day, live in rainproof houses, and have access to clean water.

CHAPTER SIX
BANKER TO THE POOR

Muhammad remembered the poor people who had stopped by his parents' house when he was a child. He remembered the homeless people and the slums he had seen when he was a Boy Scout and the starving people of Jobra he saw each day on his way to Chittagong University. And he remembered the day he met Sufiya Begum. Muhammad was grateful that he had found a way to help the poor create better lives for themselves.

Muhammad soon became known as the Banker to the Poor. Over the next few years Grameen Banks loaned more than ten billion US dollars in microcredit to almost twelve million people worldwide. Ninety-four percent of the borrowers were women.

In 2006 Muhammad Yunus and Grameen Bank were jointly awarded the Nobel Peace Prize. This prestigious award is given to an individual or a group who has shown great courage in promoting peace in countries torn apart by political **strife**, poverty, and war. The Nobel Prize committee praised Muhammad and Grameen Bank "for their efforts to create economic and social development from below" and for showing that "even the poorest of the poor can work to bring about their own development."

In his Nobel Peace Prize acceptance speech, Muhammad declared: "This year's prize gives highest honor and **dignity** to the hundreds of millions of women all around the world who struggle every day to make a living and bring hope for a better life for their children. This is a historic moment for them."

The success of Muhammad Yunus's Grameen Bank in Bangladesh has inspired many other

countries, including Russia, Israel, Saudi Arabia, Mexico, Egypt, Ghana, China, and the Philippines, to start their own **microfinance** organizations. Ninety-seven percent of Grameen Bank customers around the world have successfully paid back their loans. Grameen Bank has also awarded more than 180,000 international scholarships to poor students so they can continue their education.

According to the 2017 US **Census** Bureau statistics, the average **poverty threshold** for a family of four in the United States is an annual income of $25,094. Approximately 39.7 million people in the US — 12.3 percent of the population — live below this threshold, including 12.8 million children. To live below the poverty threshold means that a person likely does not have an adequate supply of food.

In 2008 Grameen America opened in New York City. As of 2017, the bank had opened twenty branches in thirteen cities throughout

the US. Grameen America has given loans totaling approximately a billion dollars to more than a hundred thousand women. As a result, many low-income people have been able to become financially independent and lift themselves out of poverty.

The Nobel Prize

The Nobel Prize and Nobel Peace Prize were created by a Swedish inventor and businessman named Alfred Nobel. Nobel was a chemist and engineer who invented **dynamite** and smokeless gunpowder, among many other innovations. At the time of his death in 1896, he owned almost a hundred factories in more than twenty countries and had made a huge fortune from his inventions—31.5 million Swedish crowns, which was one of the biggest fortunes in the world at the time.

Nobel never married or had children, and in his **will** he announced that all of his wealth should be invested safely to create a fund, "the interest on which shall be annually distributed in the form of prizes to those who, during the preceding year, shall have conferred *the greatest benefit on mankind.*" Nobel wanted the cash prizes to go to people working in the areas of physics, chemistry, **physiology** or medicine, literature, and peace.

Even though Nobel was Swedish, he asked the

Alfred Nobel.

Norwegian **parliament** to choose five people to form a committee to decide who would receive the prizes each year. According to his will, the Nobel Peace Prize was to be awarded *"to the person who shall have done the most or the best work for **fraternity** between the nations and the **abolition** or reduction of standing armies and the formation and spreading of **peace congresses.**"*

The Nobel Committee of the Norwegian parliament was set up in August 1897, and the first Nobel prizes were awarded in 1901. Since then, more than nine hundred individuals and twenty-four organizations have received the award, some receiving the prize more than once. The prize money varies each year, but the full Nobel Prize can be close to one million dollars. Some notable prizewinners include:

- Albert Einstein, for his services to Physics.

- Sir Alexander Fleming, awarded the prize in Physiology or Medicine for the discovery of **penicillin**, alongside two of his colleagues.

- Marie Curie, the first person to win two Nobel

Prizes: one in Physics and another in Chemistry.

- Martin Luther King, Jr., who won the Peace Prize for his work to end racial discrimination in the United States.

- Organizations such as the International Committee of the Red Cross, the United Nations International Children's Fund (UNICEF), and Amnesty International have won the Peace Prize for promoting peace, medical care, and human rights around the world.

A Norwegian stamp honoring 1992 Nobel Peace Prize laureate Rigoberta Menchú, a Guatemalan activist who fought for the rights of indigenous people.

- Malala Yousafzai, the youngest Nobel **laureate** of all, who won the Peace Prize at age seventeen for her work promoting children's rights, especially the right to an education.

Almost a year of research goes into selecting the prizewinners, and the Nobel Prizes remain the most respected awards for achievement in the world.

CHAPTER SEVEN
THE WORK CONTINUES

In 2011 the government of Bangladesh forced Muhammad Yunus to resign from Grameen Bank, stating that at more than seventy years of age, he was beyond the legal age limit to hold the position of managing director. Professor Yunus and Grameen Bank filed an **appeal** for him to continue as head of the bank, but Bangladesh's **Supreme Court** rejected the appeal. So on May 12, 2012, Muhammad Yunus officially stepped down as managing director of Grameen Bank. He now chairs the Yunus Centre and is a cofounder of Grameen Creative Lab. Both organizations have expanded beyond loaning money to the poor. They also embrace the concept of social business, promoting institutions whose primary purpose is to serve society and achieve a social goal in areas such as education, health care, nutrition, and **green energy**.

Today Muhammad Yunus lives in Bangladesh with his second wife, Afrozi Begum, a physics professor at Jahangirnagar University. His younger daughter, Deena, also lives in Bangladesh. His older daughter, Monica, from his first marriage to Vera Forostenko, is a professional opera singer who performs internationally with opera companies, including the Metropolitan Opera in New York, and other music groups.

In addition to the Nobel Peace Prize, Muhammad Yunus has received numerous other honors. Among them are the World Food Prize (1994), which recognizes individuals who have helped improve the quality, quantity, or availability of food in the world; the Sydney Peace Prize (1998), awarded by Australia for work that achieves peace with justice; the United States Presidential Medal of Freedom (2009), given to individuals for significant contributions to cultural or public works; and the Congressional Gold Medal (2010), the highest **civilian** honor for achievement by an individual or institution awarded by the US Congress. Muhammad Yunus has also received fifty honorary doctorate degrees from universities the world over to honor his contributions to the field of economics and his efforts to **eradicate** global poverty.

From helping one woman pay back her loan of twenty-two cents to providing billions of dollars in microcredit all around the world,

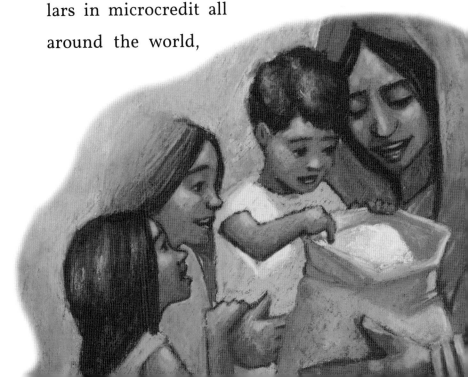

TIMELINE

1940 June 28: Muhammad Yunus born to Dula Mia and Sofia Khatun in the village of Bathua, near the city of Chittagong in Eastern Bengal, India

1947 Yunus's family moves to Chittagong to be closer to Dula Mia's business

1947 Partition roils the Indian subcontinent

1952, 1955 Yunus attends Boy Scout Jamborees in West Pakistan and Canada

1957 Yunus enrolls at Dhaka University to study economics

1960 Yunus completes his bachelor's degree in economics at Dhaka

1961 Yunus finishes his master's degree and becomes a lecturer at Chittagong University

1965 Yunus wins a Fulbright scholarship to study in the US

1969-72 Yunus works at Middle Tennessee State University in Murfreesboro, TN, as an assistant professor of economics

1970 Yunus marries Vera Forostenko

1971 Yunus receives his Ph.D. in economics from Vanderbilt University in Nashville, TN

March 25: East Pakistan declares its independence from Pakistan and establishes itself as Bangladesh. A civil war follows

December 16: The civil war ends

1972 Yunus returns to Pakistan and becomes the head of the Economics Department at Chittagong University

1974 Yunus publishes his first book, *Three Farmers of Jobra*

1976 Yunus meets Sufiya Begum and is inspired to explore microcredit

1979 Daughter Monica Yunus born; Yunus and Vera Forostenko divorce

1980 Yunus marries Afrozi Begum

1983 Grameen Bank becomes operational as an independent bank

1986 Daughter Deena Afroz Yunus born

1988 In five years, Grameen has contributed to the building of 44,556 houses, signed up nearly half a million members, and made loans totaling more than $124 million dollars.

1997 March: Grameenphone is launched as an off-shoot of Grameen Bank, in partnership with a Norwegian cell phone company. It is now the largest mobile-services provider in Bangladesh

2006 Yunus receives the Nobel Peace Prize

2009 Yunus receives the US Presidential Medal of Freedom

2010 Yunus receives the Congressional Gold Medal

2011 The government of Bangladesh forces Yunus to step down from Grameen Bank. Working with several partners, Yunus founds a company called Yunus Social Business, which offers startup funds to businesses that help address social issues around the world.

2011 Yunus becomes chancellor of Glasglow Caledonian University in Scotland, the United Kingdom, a role he fills until July 2018

GLOSSARY

abolition (ab-OH-lish-un) *noun* the act of banning or getting rid of something

appeal (ah-PEEL) *noun* in the law, an attempt to have a higher judge or court review (and usually change) the decision of a lower-ranking judge or court

bangles (BAIN-gulls) *noun* a perfectly circular bracelet

Bengali (ben-GAH-lee) *proper adjective* from the region of Bengal, a province on the eastern side of India, divided between India and East Pakistan during Partition; *noun* the language of this region

boycott (BOI-kot) *verb* to express disapproval of a person, company, or country by refusing to engage with them, especially by refusing to buy their products; *noun* the act of boycotting

breach (breech) *noun* a break or breakdown

cavalry (KAV-all-ree) *noun* soldiers who fight on horseback

census (SEN-suss) *noun* a count of all the people in a particular country. In the United States, a census is held every ten years

civilian (seh-VILL-yan) *adjective* not involved with the military or a police force

collectively (ko-LEK-tiv-lee) ad*verb* made by group effort or decision

colonize (KOL-oh-nyze) *verb* to control another country and its people, usually by imposing outside political or military rule and stealing the country's resources

courteous (KOR-tee-uss) *adjective* polite

demonstration (dem-un-STRAY-shun) *noun* a public protest against a government or ruler or for a cause

dignity (dig-NEH-tee) *noun* high respect

dilapidated (dee-LAP-ee-day-ted) *adjective* run-down, in poor repair

discriminate (duh-SKRIM-eh-nate) *verb* to act in a unfair way toward someone because of their race, ethnicity, national origin, or other personal quality

discipline (DI-seh-plen) *noun* control over oneself or others, by force or training

dynamite (DIE-nah-myt) *noun* an explosive substance used in mining and in leveling buildings or earthworks

economics (ek-oh-NAH-miks) *noun* the study of the creation and use of goods and services and other matters involving business or money

element (ELL-uh-ment) *noun* a pure chemical substance

entrepreneur (AHN-tray-PRUH-nur) *noun* a person who starts and runs a business

equivalent (ee-KWIV-ah-lent) *noun* equal

epic (eh-PIK) *adjective* grand, legendary

eradicate (ee-RAH-deh-kate) *verb* to wipe out or destroy completely

expenditures (ek-SPEN-dee-churs) *noun* the amount of money spent on buying essential and nonessential items

famine (fam-EN) *noun* a severe shortage of readily available food

fertile (FUR-tull) *adjective* good for growing things, particularly plants

fraternity (FRAH-tur-neh-tee) *noun* brotherhood

frustrated (FRUSS-tray-ted) *adjective* feeling annoyed or discouraged, often at an inability to do or accomplish something

Gandhi, Mohandas (GAHN-dee, MO-huhn-das) *person* (1869–1948) an Indian activist who led nonviolent protests against British rule; he is often called "Mahatma," which means "the Great-Souled One."

Great Depression (grate dee-PRESH-un) *proper noun* a worldwide period of economic difficulty lasting from the late 1920s to the late 1930s

green energy (green EN-er-jee) *noun* electricity that is generated in a manner that creates little to no environmental pollution—for example, wind and solar power

hinder (HIN-dur) *verb* to get in the way

Hindu (HIN-doo) *proper noun* a person who practices Hinduism, a religious tradition with roots in India that is often called the oldest religion in the world. More than one billion people identify as Hindus

hygiene (hi-JEEN) *noun* acts and behaviors that encourage good health, like cleanliness

inequality (IN-ee-KWAL-eh-tee) *noun* the state of being unequal

inflict (in-FLIKT) *verb* to force something painful or unwanted on another being

investment (in-VEST-ment) *noun* money spent with a strategy for making more money from it long term; for example, if you opened a lemonade stand, the money spent buying lemons and sugar would be an investment

jamboree (jam-buh-REE) *noun* a party involving many people and often lasting several days

laureate (LOR-ee-ate) *noun* the winner of a prize for significant achievements

microfinance (MY-kro-fy-NANS) *noun* banking services provided to the poor, often in the form of small loans known as *microloans* or *microcredit*

minimize (MIN-eh-myze) *verb* to make something as small as possible

Muslim (MUZ-lim) *proper noun* a person who practices Islam, including nearly a quarter of the world population

negotiations (nee-GO-she-A-shuns) *noun* the act of talking to another person or party to reach an agreement

parliament (PAR-lah-ment) *noun* the national legislature in some countries, much like the US Congress

peace congresses (peese KON-gress-ez) *plural noun* conferences in which representatives of countries around the world come together to resolve their differences

penicillin (PEN-ee-SILL-en) *noun* a kind of mold that can hinder the growth of bacteria, and is therefore used in many drugs that prevent or stop infections

pit latrine (pit la-TREEN) *noun* a toilet constructed by digging a deep hole underground and then placing a platform or seat over it

physiology (FIZ-ee-OLL-oh-jee) *noun* the study of the workings and processes of living things

poverty (PAH-ver-tee) *noun* a situation of lack, particularly lacking money or other resources

poverty threshold (PAH-ver-tee THRESH-old) *noun* a specific amount of income thought to be the amount necessary to meet a family's basic needs

prestigious (preh-STIJ-us) *adjective* having respect from or importance to other people

prime minister (prym mih-NEE-ster) *noun* the official leader of a country with a parliament

principal (prins-EE-pal) *noun* in financial terms, the beginning sum of money that a customer either saves in or borrows from a bank.

profit (PROFF-it) *noun* the money made from a business deal after the costs have been subtracted; *verb* to make a profit

prosperity (pro-SPARE-eh-tee) *noun* success, especially through making a large amount of money

purdah (PUR-duh) *noun* the practice of keeping the male and female genders separate, especially common in conservative Hindu or Muslim communities

purify (pyur-ee-fy) *verb* to make something clean or pure

refugees (reh-FEW-jeez) *plural noun* people who leave their homes in search of safety

rickshaw (RIK-shah) *noun* a vehicle that usually carries one passenger, who sits on a seat over two wheels on the same axle and is then pulled along by one person

secede (suh-SEED) *verb* to withdraw from a larger group

Second Boer War (BOH-er war) *proper noun* a war that lasted from October 1899 to May 1902 between the British Empire and two former Dutch colonies in the area that is now South Africa

sewage (SOO-idge) *noun* liquid waste, especially human waste

shanties (SHAN-tees) *plural noun* small, poorly built or run-down houses

siege (seej) *noun* a sustained attack on a town or other stronghold during a war

Sikh (seek) *proper noun* a person who practices Sikhism, a religion founded in India in the 1500s with nearly 25 million followers

sit-ins (sit-inz) *plural noun* protests in which a group of activists sit down in a public area and refuse to leave

slums (slumz) *noun* an area noted for its poverty within a larger city, including poor housing, crowded conditions, and little economic opportunity

strife (stryf) *noun* fighting or other conflict

subcontinent (sub-KON-tee-nint) a large area of land thought to be distinct within a larger continent due to its unique geography or culture

Supreme Court (soo-PREEM kort) *proper noun* the highest court of law in a country

surplus (sur-PLUSS) *noun* an extra amount; a remainder or leftover

taka (TAH-kuh) *proper noun* the unit of money in Bangladesh. One taka is usually worth about one cent in United States money

trudge (truhj) *verb* to walk with a slow and heavy step

turmoil (TER-moy-ull) *noun* trouble

Vietnam War (vee-et-NOM wor) *proper noun* a war lasting from 1954 to 1975 in which South Vietnamese and United States forces tried to keep Communist North Vietnam from taking over South Vietnam. The United States ultimately withdrew and North Vietnam unified the country

weary (WEER-ee) *adjective* tired, exhausted

will (will) *noun* a document in which a person specifies what should be done with their money and possessions after their death

woodcraft (wood-kraft) *noun* activities useful for surviving in the woods, like hunting, fishing, and using a compass

AUTHOR'S SOURCES

"Bangladesh and Pakistan: The Forgotten War." TIME Photos. http://content.time.com/time/photogallery/0,29307,1844754,00.html.

Bornstein, David. *The Price of a Dream: The Story of the Grameen Bank.* New York: Oxford University Press, 2005.

Grameen America. http://grameenamerica.org/.

Grameen Bank: Bank for the Poor. http://www.grameen-info.org/ and http://www.grameen.com.

"Microcredit Pioneers Win Nobel Peace Prize." *USA Today*/Associated Press, October 13, 2006. http://www.usatoday.com/news/world/2006-10-13-norway-nobel_x.htm.

Nichols, Michelle. "'Banker to the Poor' Gives New York Women a Boost." Reuters, April 23, 2009. http://www.reuters.com/article/domesticNews/idUSTRE53M13G20090423?rpc=46.

"The Nobel Peace Prize 2006: Muhammad Yunus, Grameen Bank." Nobelprize.org, February 2014. http://www.nobelprize.org/nobel_prizes/peace/laureates/2006.

Reitz, Hans. "The Grameen Creative Lab—What Is It?" PDF presentation given to the author, May 2009.

Siddiqi, Samana. "Statistics on Poverty and Food Wastage in America." SoundVision.com. http://www.soundvision.com/Info/poor/statistics.asp.

"What Are Poverty Thresholds and Poverty Guidelines?" Institute for Research on Poverty: University of Wisconsin-Madison. http://www.irp.wisc.edu/resources/what-are-poverty-thresholds-and-poverty-guidelines.

Wight, Vanessa R. , Michelle Chau, and Yumiko Aratani. "Who Are America's Poor Children? The Official Story." NCCP: National Center for Children in Poverty, January 2010. http://www.nccp.org/publications/pub_912.html#1.

Yunus, Muhammad. "Nobel Lecture." The Nobel Prize. Oslo, Norway, December 10, 2006. http://www.nobelprize.org/nobel_prizes/peace/laureates/2006/yunus-lecture-en.html.

———. Personal interview with the author. Los Angeles, CA: Westin Hotel, May 24, 2009.

———, and Alan Jolis. *Banker to the Poor: Micro-Lending and the Battle Against World Poverty.* New York: Public Affairs, 1999.

Statistics about Grameen Bank were provided to the author by the Yunus Centre.

QUOTATION SOURCES

p. 11: "Learning from . . . greatest learning." Muhammad Yunus interview with the author. Westin Hotel, Los Angeles, CA, May 24, 2009.

p. 55: "[F]or their efforts . . . development from below." Quoted in "The Nobel Peace Prize for 2006" news release, October 13, 2006. The Nobel Prize. https://www.nobelprize.org/prizes/peace/2006/press-release/.

"[E]ven the poorest . . . own development." Ibid.

"This year's prize . . . moment for them." Quoted in Muhammad Yunus, "Nobel Lecture," presented at the Nobel Prize ceremony, December 10, 2006. The Nobel Prize. https://www.nobelprize.org/prizes/peace/2006/ceremony-speech/.

SIDEBAR SOURCES

THE BOY SCOUTS

Baden-Powell, Robert. *Scouting for Boys.* Oxford: Oxford University Press, 2005.

Boy Scouts of America. "Scouting Programs." Accessed November 1, 2018. https://www.scouting.org/programs/.

Collis, Henry, Fred Hurll, and Rex Hazlewood. *B.-P.'s Scouts, An Official History of The Boy Scouts Association.* London: Collins, 1961.

Moynihan, Paul. *An Official History of Scouting.* Foreword by Lord Robert Baden-Powell. London: Hamlyn, 2006.

The New Encyclopedia Britannica. 15th Edition. London: Encyclopedia Britannica Inc., 2002.

Reuters. "US Boy Scouts to Change Name in Appeal to Girls." Accessed October 30, 2018. https://www.reuters.com/article/us-usa-scouts/u-s-boy-scouts-to-change-name-in-appeal-to-girls-idUSKBN1I32EQ.

The Scout Association. "BADEN-POWELL: Chief Scout of the World." Accessed September 11, 2018. http://scouts.org.uk/media/52831/baden_powell.pdf.

———. "The Scout Association's programme objectives." Accessed November 1, 2018. https://members. scouts.org.uk/documents/6to25/Programme%20 Objectives%20-%20FINAL%20(rebrand).pdf.

The Scouting Pages. "Brownsea Island – The First Camp." Accessed October 31, 2018. https://thescoutingpages. org.uk/the-first-camp/.

Scouts South Africa. "The Mafeking Cadets." Accessed October 31, 2018. http://www.scouting.org.za/seeds/ cadets.html.

World Organization of the Scout Movement. "National Scout Organizations." Accessed November 8, 2018. https://www.scout.org/worldwide.

THE PARTITION OF INDIA AND THE CREATION OF BANGLADESH

Bbc.co.uk. "Bangladesh Profile – Timeline." Last updated February 29, 2019. https://www.bbc.co.uk/news/ world-south-asia-12651483.

Bojang, Ali Brownlie. *India.* Countries Around the World. London: Heinemann-Raintree, 2013.

Bojang, Ali Brownlie, and Nicola Barber. *Focus on India.* World in Focus. London: Wayland/Hachette, 2006.

Commonwealth Secretariat. "Bangladesh: History." Accessed September 12, 2018. http://thecommonwealth.org/ our-member-countries/bangladesh/history.

Dalrymple, William. "The Great Divide: the violent legacy of Indian Partition." *The New Yorker,* June 29, 2015. Accessed November 3, 2018. https:// www.newyorker.com/magazine/2015/06/29/ the-great-divide-books-dalrymple.

Encyclopaedia Britannica. "European Expansion Since 1763." Accessed November 2, 2018. https:// www.britannica.com/topic/colonialism/ European-expansion-since-1763.

———. "Massacre of Amritsar." Accessed November 2, 2018. https://www.britannica.com/event/ Massacre-of-Amritsar.

Henderson, Barney. "Indian Independence Day: everything you need to know about Partition between India and Pakistan 70 years on." *The Telegraph*, August 15, 2017. Accessed November 3, 2018. https://www.telegraph.co.uk/news/2017/08/15/ indian-independence-day-everything- need-know-partition-india/.

The New Internationalist. "Bangladesh A Brief History." Last updated March 5, 2001. Accessed September 12, 2018. https://newint.org/features/2001/03/05/ history.

Open University, The. "Choudhary Rahmat Ali."
Accessed November 2, 2018. http://www.open.
ac.uk/researchprojects/makingbritain/content/
choudhary-rahmat-ali.

Sinha-Kerkhoff, Kathunka. *Tyranny of Partition: Hindus
in Bangladesh & Muslims in India.* New Delhi: Gyan
Publishing House, 2006.

Visit Bangladesh. "History of Bangladesh." Accessed
September 12, 2018. https://visitbangladesh.gov.bd/
about-bangladesh/history-of-bangladesh/.

White, Bender Richardson. *Facts About Countries:
Bangladesh.* London: Franklin Watts, 2005.

HOW BANKS MAKE MONEY

Coppola, Frances. "How Bank Lending Really Creates
Money, And Why The Magic Money Tree is Not
Cost Free." Forbes.com. Published October 31, 2017.
Accessed September 12, 2018. https://www.forbes.
com/sites/francescoppola/2017/10/31/how-bank-
lending-really-creates-money-and-why-the-magic-
money-tree-is-not-cost-free/#f91d6ea3073e.

Hall, Alvin. *Show Me The Money: Big Questions About
Finance.* New York: Dorling Kindersley, 2016.

Hazlitt, Henry. *Economics in One Lesson.* New York: Three
Rivers Press, 1946.

How Money Works: The Facts Visually Explained. New York: Dorling Kindersley Limited, 2017.

McLay, Michael, Amar Radia, and Ryland Thomas. "Money Creation in the Modern Economy." Bank of England. Published March 14, 2014. Accessed September 13, 2018. https://www. bankofengland.co.uk/quarterly-bulletin/2014/q1/ money-creation-in-the-modern-economy.

Patin, Hillary. "How Do Banks Make Money?" Simple. com. Accessed September 12, 2018. https://www.simple.com/blog/ how-do-banks-make-money.

SIXTEEN DECISIONS

Arman, Shaila, Leanne Unicomb, and Stephen P. Luby. "A Qualitative Exploration of Factors Affecting Uptake of Water Treatment Technology in Rural Bangladesh," in *When Culture Impacts Health: Global Lessons for Effective Health Research.* Abstract accessed November 6, 2018. https://www.sciencedirect.com/ science/article/pii/B978012415921100018X.

Discoverybangladesh.com. "Bangladesh: Land, Resources and Natural Regions." Accessed September 19, 2018. http://www.discoverybangla-desh.com/meetbangladesh/land_resources.html.

———. "People and Population of Bangladesh." Accessed September 19, 2018. http://www.discoverybangladesh.com/meetbangladesh/people.html.

Grameen.com. "Breaking the Vicious Cycle of Poverty Through Microcredit." Accessed November 6, 2018. http://www.grameen.com/breaking-the-cycle-of-proverty/.

———. "16 Decisions." Accessed September 13, 2018. http://www.grameen.com/16-decisions/.

———. "10 Indicators." Accessed September 21, 2018. http://www.grameen.com/10-indicators/.

Robert F. Kennedy Human Rights. "Muhammad Yunus." Accessed September 13, 2018. https://rfkhumanrights.org/assets/documents/Muhammad-Yunus.pdf.

ScienceDirect. "Potassium Alum." Accessed November 6, 2018. https://www.sciencedirect.com/topics/pharmacology-toxicology-and-pharmaceutical-science/potassium-alum.

Thryn, Damien. "How to Use Powdered Alum to Purify Water." Accessed November 6, 2018. https://sciencing.com/use-powdered-alum-purify-water-7411961.html.

White, Bender Richardson. *Facts About Countries: Bangladesh*. London: Franklin Watts, 2005.

Yunus Centre. "About Yunus Centre." Accessed
September 18, 2018. http://www.muhammadyunus.
org/index.php/yunus-centre/about-yunus-centre.

THE NOBEL PRIZE

Britannica.com. "Nobel Prize Award." Accessed
September 17, 2018. https://www.britannica.com/
topic/Nobel-Prize.

The Nobel Peace Prize. "History." Accessed September 17,
2018. https://www.nobelpeaceprize.org/History.

The Nobel Prize. "Alfred Nobel – His Life and Work."
Accessed September 24, 2018.
https://www.nobelprize.org/alfred-nobel/
alfred-nobels-life-and-work/.

———. "All Nobel Prizes." Accessed November 6,
2018. https://www.nobelprize.org/prizes/lists/
all-nobel-prizes/.

———. "The Nobel Prize Amounts." Accessed November
6, 2018. https://www.nobelprize.org/prizes/about/
the-nobel-prize-amounts/.

———. "Nobel Prize Facts." Accessed November 6,
2018. https://www.nobelprize.org/prizes/facts/
nobel-prize-facts/.

RECOMMENDED READING

Fiction books are marked with an asterisk (*).

SCOUTING

Acevedo, Sylvia. *Path to the Stars: My Journey from Girl Scout to Rocket Scientist.* New York: Clarion Books, 2018.

Birkby, Robert. *Boy Scouts of America Scout Stuff: A Centennial History of Scouting Memorabilia.* New York: Dorling Kindersley, 2011.

Boy Scouts of America and J. Wayne Fears. *The Scouting Guide to Survival: An Official Boy Scouts of America Handbook: More than 200 Essential Skills for Staying Warm, Building a Shelter, and Signaling for Help.* New York: Skyhorse, 2018.

Corey, Shana. *Here Come the Girl Scouts!: The Amazing All-True Story of Juliette "Daisy" Gordon Low and Her Great Adventure.* Illustrated by Hadley Hooper. New York: Scholastic Press, 2012.

Girl Scouts of the USA and Betty Christiansen. *Girl Scouts: A Celebration of 100 Amazing Years.* New York: Stewart, Tabori and Chang, 2011.

Wadsworth, Ginger. *First Girl Scout: The Life of Juliette Gordon Low.* New York: Clarion Books, 2012.

Wills, Chuck. *Boy Scouts of America: A Centennial History*. New York: Dorling Kindersley, 2013.

THE INDIAN STRUGGLE FOR INDEPENDENCE AND PARTITION

* Hiranandani, Veera. *The Night Diary*. New York: Dial Books, 2018.

* Kelkar, Supriya. *Ahimsa*. New York: Tu Books, 2017.

Rau, Dana Meachan. *Who Was Gandhi?* Who Was series. Illustrated by Jerry Hoare. New York: Penguin Workshop, 2014.

BANKING & MONEY

* Clements, Andrew. *Lunch Money*. New York: Atheneum/ Simon & Schuster, 2005.

* Davies, Jacqueline. *The Lemonade War*. New York: Houghton Mifflin Harcourt, 2007.

* Flake, Sharon. *Money Hungry*. New York: Jump at the Sun/Hyperion Books for Children, 2001.

* Frazier, Sundee. *Cleo Edison Oliver: Playground Millionaire*. New York: Arthur A. Levine Books/Scholastic, 2016.

Furgang, Kathy. *Everything Money*. Washington, D.C.: National Geographic Kids, 2013.

Hall, Alvin. *Show Me The Money: Big Questions About Finance*. New York: Dorling Kindersley, 2016.

Karlitz, Gail, and Debbie Honig. *Growing Money: A Complete Investment Guide for Kids*. New York: Price Stern Sloan, 2010.

McKenna, James, Jeannine Glista, and Matt Fontaine. *How to Turn $100 into $1,000,000: Earn! Save! Invest!* New York: Workman, 2016.

BANGLADESH

White, Bender Richardson. *Facts About Countries: Bangladesh*. London: Franklin Watts, 2005.

ABOUT THE AUTHOR AND ILLUSTRATOR

PAULA YOO is an author and screenwriter whose other children's books for Lee & Low include *Sixteen Years in Sixteen Seconds*, *Shining Star*, and several titles in the Confetti Kids series. Her titles have been recognized by the International Reading Association, the Texas Bluebonnet Award Master List, and Lee & Low's New Voices Award. She and her husband live in Los Angeles, California, where she works in television. You can visit her website at paulayoo.com.

JAMEL AKIB is an award-winning illustrator whose work has appeared in several picture books as well as in numerous museum and gallery shows in England, including several Best of British Illustration exhibitions. A full-time illustrator of English and Malaysian ancestry, Akib now lives with his family in Salisbury, England.